MANA &
INSOMNIA IN THE
OLDER PERSON

Kevin Morgan & Ken Gledhill

With additional material by Maureen Tomeny

WINSLOW PRESS

Telford Road, Bicester, Oxon OX6 0TS

First published in 1991 by
Winslow Press, Telford Road, Bicester, Oxon OX6 0TS

Phototypeset by Gecko Limited, Bicester, Oxon
02-1295/Printed in Great Britain by Hobbs the Printers,
Southampton

British Library Cataloguing in Publication Data
Morgan, Kevin
Managing sleep and insomnia in the older person
I. Title   II. Gledhill, Ken   III. Tomeny, Maureen
612.8210880565

ISBN 0-86388-094-0

MANAGING SLEEP & INSOMNIA IN THE OLDER PERSON

To our parents, partners and children

Contents

KEVIN MORGAN BSc PhD is a lecturer in gerontology in the Department of Health Care of the Elderly, University of Nottingham Medical School.

KEN GLEDHILL BA MSc is a top grade clinical psychologist with Huddersfield Health Authority.

MAUREEN TOMENY MA MSc is a principal clinical psychologist with Central Nottinghamshire Health Authority.

Preface —
Using this Book

Books dealing with clinical issues in later life are often written for specific professional groups (eg. psychologists, nurses, doctors) and, not infrequently, focus on specific sections of the older population (perhaps the very frail, or those in residential care). The reasons for this are obvious enough. Certain issues concern some professionals more than others, or pertain to some older people more than others. Insomnia, however, is neither easily nor usefully confined within such boundaries. Sleep problems affect all kinds of older people — the active and the inactive, the independent and the dependent, the frail and the otherwise healthy, those in their sixties and those in their nineties. Similarly, the management of sleep problems involves all those with a professional responsibility for the health of older people, whether in primary care, hospital or residential settings.

This book, then, has not been written with any particular professional group in mind. Instead, we have adopted a problem-centred approach, placing the emphasis on what can be done, rather than on who should do it. This choice of emphasis has implications both for how the information is presented, and how it should be approached. As for presentation, we have tried to organize material in a sequence which, chapter by chapter, moves from the less specialized to the more specialized components of management. One effect of this is that while earlier chapters will apply to most client and professional groups, later chapters refer to therapeutic approaches applicable to clients with particular problems, and professionals with particular skills. Nevertheless, on the assumption that the information alone will be helpful to all those who participate in management, we have written this book to be read as a whole. If you are professionally interested in sleep problems in later life, and think this book may be of value, then our advice to you is the same as that offered to the White Rabbit by the King of Hearts: "Begin at the beginning, and go on till you come to the end: then stop."

One further point on presentation. While the later chapters concern more specialized approaches to management, they are also less detailed. The assumption here is that those in a position to offer these therapies will already possess the necessary basic skills. What we aim to provide in the text is specific guidance on the use of these techniques in the treatment of sleep problems in older people. It should also be noted that all of the information presented here is based on research and clinical experience. Rather than clutter the pages with footnotes or citations, a selected bibliography is provided at the end of the text. For those unfamiliar with the research in this area, we hope this will provide a useful introduction to a fascinating and rapidly growing literature.

Finally, we are pleased to acknowledge our gratitude to Maureen Tomeny for allowing us to include and modify her therapeutic materials in *Chapters 6 and 12.*

Section 1
Understanding
Insomnia

1
Approaching Sleep Problems

Good sleep is essential for maintaining physical and psychological well-being at any age. Unfortunately, later life is often accompanied by a variety of factors which, one way or another, have a detrimental effect on sleep quality. At a time when personal resources are especially taxed by, for example, retirement, periods of illness, bereavement or the demands of caring, persistently disturbed sleep can progressively erode health, morale and the stamina necessary to cope.

Yet despite this, the management of insomnia in older people is widely misunderstood. Indeed, it might appear (both to clients and health professionals alike) that, apart from sleeping tablets, there is little that can be offered to the older insomniac. This is far from being the case. Numerous practical responses, ranging from self-help advice through to more individualized treatments, are known to be effective in the management of late-life sleep problems. Importantly, such responses are not confined to any particular group of professionals or carers. On the contrary, the management of insomnia among older people is ideally suited to a broad interdisciplinary approach, with different health care professionals contributing whatever their experience and training allows. The aim of this book is to provide guidance on how to organize such a response, and to encourage the broadest possible professional involvement in the management of a widespread and serious health problem.

PRINCIPLES OF MANAGEMENT

Sleep problems in later life are rarely simple matters. Nevertheless, however complex the problem, and whatever its cause, the key to successful management lies in a structured and sensitive approach. Time is less likely to be wasted, and management more likely to be effective, if the sleep problem is carefully assessed, if interventions are carefully selected and if outcomes are carefully monitored. These three steps — *A*ssessment, *I*ntervention and *M*onitoring — can be summarized in the acronym AIM, and provide the basis of the clinical approach described in this book.

Effective management also requires two other important ingredients. The first is an understanding of normal sleep; the second is a working knowledge of the possible causes of sleep disturbance. Unfortunately, over the years both topics have attracted more than their fair share of myths and half truths. It is unhelpful if an elderly client has a distorted view of what constitutes 'good' sleep. It is doubly unhelpful if that view is shared or encouraged by health professionals. Before discussing therapeutic approaches, therefore, some consideration will first be given to facts about sleep and insomnia in later life. In addition to helping professionals understand the nature of sleep problems, these facts, presented in the following two chapters, can also be used as the basis for information and advice initially offered to clients.

SUMMARY

The approach to managing insomnia set out in this book is based upon three separate steps: *assessment* of the sleep problem, targeted *intervention* and the ongoing *monitoring* of outcomes.

2
Understanding Sleep

Patterns of sleep change whether we are growing up or growing old. Newborn babies, for example, spend about 16–17 hours fast asleep each day. Children aged three to five years sleep for about 11 hours, while teenagers average about eight to nine hours each night. By the age of 30 years, many people are sleeping for less than eight hours, and many 50-year-olds average only six hours per night. For many people, then, reductions in the length of their sleep continue throughout life.

Nevertheless, while the length of time spent asleep is clearly important, it is not the only (nor, often, the most important) aspect of sleep to change. Two other influential changes also accompany ageing: sleep becomes lighter and more broken. Both are related to alterations in the fundamental structure of human sleep and are explained below.

AGEING AND THE STRUCTURE OF SLEEP

During sleep our bodies and brains show quite distinct patterns of activity. On the basis of this activity, sleep can be divided into five separate stages: the REM stage (REM, usually pronounced as a word, stands for rapid eye movement because during this stage the eyes tend to dart about beneath closed lids); and four non-REM or NREM stages, simply called Stage 1, Stage 2, Stage 3 and Stage 4.

One of the many differences between these stages is their depth. It requires quite a lot of noise, for example, to wake someone from Stage 4 sleep, slightly less noise to wake someone from Stage 3, and less noise again to wake someone from Stage 2. The REM stage is a rather special case (it is during this stage that we do most of our vivid dreaming), but it is about as deep as Stage 4.

During sleep these stages follow in turn (like a descending staircase): Stage 1 (drowsiness), is followed by Stage 2 (light sleep), which, depending upon how old you are, is followed by Stages 3 and 4 (deep sleep). The order then reverses, and sleep becomes lighter as Stage 4 is followed by Stages 3 and 2. A REM period may then follow, after which the whole sequence can start again. A complete sequence (ie, light sleep — deeper sleep — lighter sleep — REM) is called a 'cycle' and, in young adults, takes about 90–100 minutes to complete. Several cycles can be completed in a single night and sometimes, during the lighter parts of the cycle, we awaken spontaneously for a moment or two before returning to sleep.

With increasing age the amount of deep sleep (ie, Stages 3 and 4) tends to diminish, while periods of light sleep and drowsiness tend to increase. In normal healthy middle-aged and elderly people very deep sleep (Stage 4) can actually disappear altogether. As mentioned above, the effect of these changes is that sleep becomes lighter and more broken, with both the likelihood of being disturbed, and the likelihood of awakening spontaneously tending to increase. Put another way, older sleep is not only shorter, but is also more restless and more fragile.

AGEING AND THE BIOLOGICAL CLOCK

Advancing age also influences the biological clock which controls the timing of sleep. In later life the strength of the connection between this biological clock and the clock on the mantelpiece begins to weaken, resulting in, among other things, a tendency to sleep during the day (napping is discussed in greater detail in *Chapter 8*). Disruptions of the habitual sleep–wake patterns are also less well tolerated in later life. Older people find it more difficult to cope with the effects of jet-lag, or to take sleep loss in their stride.

WELL-BEING AND SLEEP

In addition to the changes described so far, increasing age can also usher in a variety of events which can affect the quality of sleep indirectly. Sometimes these events are minor in themselves but, in combination with existing age-related changes, can represent the 'last straw'. For example, the need to empty the bladder during the night (nocturia) becomes quite common in later life. (About 60% of women, and about 70% of men, aged over 65 leave their beds at least once during the night to go to the toilet.) In itself, this is not a problem; most people can, after all, cope with one or two night-time excursions. Getting up for the toilet can become a problem if, on returning to bed, the individual experiences difficulty in getting back to sleep. Sometimes, however, these 'additional' events are of such major personal significance that they would probably create a sleep problem at any age. The emotional trauma of bereavement, or the joint pains associated with arthritis, provide two examples.

As a guide, examples of some of the more common factors which can disturb sleep in later life are shown below in *Figure 2.1* under three headings: medical, psychological and personal factors. Medical problems can influence sleep through pain and discomfort, but can also be a cause of worry and stress. Specific medicines, too, can also interfere with sleep (*see Chapter 8*).

Sleep is particularly sensitive to psychological disturbance, with anxiety, depression and dementing illness all having a characteristically disruptive influence. Anxiety, as most of us will know, tends to affect the ability to get to sleep. Depression, on the other hand, can often affect the ability to stay asleep. In dementia the age-related changes in sleep structure described above appear to be amplified. Elderly people with dementing illness show patterns of light, fragmented sleep, often accompanied by excessive daytime napping. In severe cases the 24-hour sleep–wake pattern can break down altogether, with sleep being as likely during the day as during the night. These particular problems will be dealt with in *Chapter 14*.

Finally, an individual's personal circumstances can often have a marked effect on sleep quality. Older people, for example, are more likely to sleep in colder bedrooms and older beds, neither of which are helpful if sleep becomes disturbed. Disruption of sleep is also a quite normal response to an abrupt change in the sleep environment. Under most circumstances, therefore, periods of institutionalization can be expected, at least at first, to affect even a robust sleeping pattern.

Medical (Physical Health)	Psychological (Mental Health)	Personal
Nocturia Limb cramps Breathing difficulties Prescribed medicines	Anxiety Depression Dementia	Bereavement Loneliness Poor sleep environment Institutionalization

Figure 2.1 **Common Factors Which Can Disturb Sleep in Later Life**

SUMMARY

With advancing age normal sleep tends to become shorter, lighter and more broken. In addition, sleep can be disturbed by the changes in health and personal circumstances which frequently accompany the process of ageing. All of these factors can contribute to insomnia.

3

About Insomnia

On the basis of the changes looked at so far, it is very tempting to conclude that older people simply need less sleep than younger people. Certainly the total amount of time spent asleep tends to diminish in later life (even when daytime napping is taken into account). However, this in itself certainly does not mean that sleep is any less important — after all, nobody suggests that eyesight gets worse with age because older people need to see less. There are no hard and fast rules about how much sleep a person needs. But one thing is certain, sleep remains essential whether we are 18 or 80.

HOW MUCH SLEEP DO WE NEED?

How, then, do people know if they are getting enough sleep? Individuals differ widely in the amount of sleep they feel they need, and these differences tend to become even greater as we get older. For example, some 60-year-olds might still enjoy seven hours sleep each night, while others might feel satisfied with five hours or less. What really matters here is quality rather than quantity. Sleep which leaves people feeling alert, refreshed and able to cope is 'good sleep', while sleep which leaves people feeling tired, 'washed-out' and inefficient is not 'good sleep'.

This has some important implications. It may be that while some older people are refreshed by shorter sleep, they may nevertheless feel frustrated by having to endure longer periods of wakefulness early in the morning. Though people frequently think of this situation as a sleep problem, it may be more helpful to view it as a 'wake' problem, and respond accordingly.

WHAT IS INSOMNIA?

For the most part, this book will deal with only one, though probably the most common, type of sleep disturbance — insomnia. Technically, insomnia refers to problems of *getting* to sleep (sleep onset insomnia) or problems of *staying* asleep (sleep maintenance insomnia). Often these problems are expressed in the subjective complaint of poor quality or restless sleep. Alternatively, a sleep problem may be observed in others by a partner or carer, or perhaps inferred from a person's sleepiness during the day. Whatever the case, each provides a point of departure for structured assessment.

Primary and Secondary Insomnia

Insomnias can also be categorized as *primary* or *secondary*. Primary insomnias are those which seem to arise spontaneously, and are not related to any known illness or disability. Secondary insomnias, on the other hand, are related to illness or psychological problems and may remit when the underlying problem itself responds to treatment. (This does not always happen, and many insomniacs can trace a persistent sleep problem back to a period of illness from which they have long since recovered.) Whether primary or secondary, most insomnias can be appropriately managed using the behavioural strategies and techniques described in this book. The important difference is that the management of secondary sleep problems must be accompanied by appropriate treatment for the underlying disorder.

On Subjective Complaints

The management of insomnia is both initiated and guided by subjective assessments. This subjectivity is sometimes a source of concern among health professionals perhaps more accustomed to objective, tangible evidence of underlying disorder and subsequent improvement. It should be kept in mind, however, that the clinical management of wholly subjective states is not particularly unusual. Complaints of pain, for example (which are equally subjective), are usually taken at face value. Furthermore, reports of pain tend to produce a structured response which aims to identify the site, type, severity and so on of the complaint before treatment is commenced. A similar approach to sleep complaints is, therefore, quite appropriate.

Insomnia and Ageing

It is not just the objective characteristics of sleep (its length, depth etc) which change as people get older. With advancing age, satisfaction with sleep also tends to decline and, as if to reinforce the point, the consumption of sleeping tablets shows a steady and reciprocal increase. Among elderly people living at home about one in four has a sleep problem, while about one in eight regularly consumes sleeping tablets. Overall, problems of staying asleep (sleep maintenance insomnia) appear to be more common than problems of getting to sleep (sleep onset insomnia), though many clients complain of both.

Sleep problems also tend to be more persistent in later life, often lasting for months and years rather than days or weeks. This is a particularly important point. Among younger people, insomnia is often a transient affair, remitting when circumstances change. Among older clients, sleep is simply more fragile, and problems which are left unmanaged, or which are mismanaged, often become progressively worse before becoming entrenched. The systematic management of insomnia, therefore, represents both a practical response to a current problem and an investment in the future well-being of elderly clients. Before moving on to discuss this response, however, the next chapter will focus briefly on who does what.

SUMMARY

Insomnia, the subjective complaint of poor sleep, becomes more common with increasing age. Problems of getting to sleep are called sleep onset insomnias, while problems of staying asleep are called sleep maintenance insomnias. Both are common in later life.

4
Helping with Sleep Problems

Inevitably, multidisciplinary approaches to health care problems introduce the issue of professional boundaries. In a team everybody cannot do everything. While the existence of boundaries between different health professionals may be established by training, tradition or the law, recognition of these boundaries often results mainly from practical experience. A nurse, for example, will use experience to judge when palliative responses to pain should give way to a request for prescribed analgesia. Similarly, a general practitioner will use experience to decide when the management of a person's depression should be passed to a psychologist or psychiatrist. Unfortunately, the interdisciplinary management of sleep is less well established. Consequently, individual health workers may not only be unaware of what they themselves can offer, they may also be unaware of what help can be shared.

WHAT CAN YOU OFFER AND WHAT CAN YOU SHARE?

The approach to sleep problems described in the following chapters includes aspects of health education, behavioural management and psychological therapy. It is up to individual readers to decide which areas of management fall within their own professional boundaries. Having said that, it is also important to emphasize that many of the responses outlined here are intended to run in parallel, not in series. That is, as each new component of management is introduced, earlier components are continued. As a general rule, less specialized responses (which require lower levels of skill) are introduced early in management, while more specialized responses (which need higher levels of skill) are introduced later. This is illustrated in *Figure 4.1* below. Points concerning the overall structure of management will be taken up in the next section.

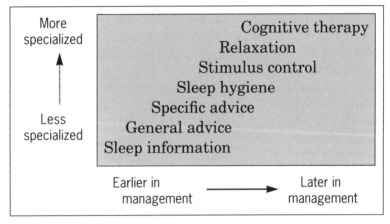

Figure 4.1 **Responses to sleep problems**

Section 2
Responding to Insomnia

5
First Things First

Before attempting to manage the problem, it is a useful investment of time if the style, aims and details of the approach to be used are first discussed with the client. The following three points are intended as guidelines for this first step.

SETTING REALISTIC GOALS

It is particularly important, both for the credibility of health professionals and the well-being of older clients, that the goals of management are clearly understood. Simply put, the aim is not to cure insomnia, but to improve sleep quality. This can be made clear to the client in quite positive terms by emphasizing the likelihood of improvement (rather than emphasizing the likelihood of no cure). This aim can be expressed in another way. Quite often it is the sheer unpredictability of sleep which is soul-destroying for chronic insomniacs — not knowing if they are going to lie awake for hours or fall asleep exhausted. Successful management may not restore perfect sleep, but it will help to make sleeping patterns more reliable. And very often that is enough.

It is also important to realize that a problem successfully managed at one point in time can return at another. This, however, serves to illustrate one of the strengths of the approach described here. If put into practice, self-help and psychological strategies equip the client to deal more effectively with both present and future problems.

OVERCOMING RESISTANCE

Usually successful management is impossible without the cooperation and effort of the client (one exception to this is the management of sleep problems in dementia). Nevertheless, active participation in treatment, particularly when it means doing things which are temporarily inconvenient, can meet with resistance. Keep in mind that, for many years, sleeping tablets have dominated the management of insomnia and that active participation in management may, to some clients, seem rather unorthodox. Naturally the client has the right to choose not to cooperate; behavioural approaches do not suit everybody. If, however, you wish to offer encouragement, then it might be useful to point out: (a) that if cooperating is really no worse than the problem, then what has the client to lose?; and (b) that for a number of reasons sleep problems in later life tend to get worse over time, and that a little inconvenience now may prevent a lot of inconvenience later.

UNDERSTANDING THE STRUCTURED RESPONSE

The overall strategy described in this book is based on the sequence: *A*ssess the problem, then *I*ntervene, and then *M*onitor the outcome of intervention (AIM). Within this strategy there is another guiding principle: manage the simpler issues first. In this way the response can build up in a logical and practical way. If sufficient improvement is obtained with relatively simple interventions, the more complex can be avoided. This is just common sense. For example, imagine a car that refuses to start. It is reasonable to check simple things (does it need petrol? is the anti-theft device still switched on? is the battery flat? are the sparking plugs wet? etc) before calling for time-consuming and perhaps expensive assistance.

There is another reason for responding in this way. Sometimes different factors underlying insomnia (or engine failure) cause problems only when they act together. Returning to the car example, a less-than-lively battery may only be a problem when the spark plugs need cleaning. Similarly, drinking two pints of strong black coffee every day might become a problem only if some further factor (pain, illness, ageing itself) starts to disturb sleep. A broad systematic approach to management can help to interrupt such interactions, and optimize improvement.

SUMMARY

Successful management is generally impossible without the cooperation of the client. A brief preliminary discussion with the client should aim to set realistic goals, overcome resistance and explain simply the overall approach.

6

Assessing Sleep

Having discussed the approach, assessment of the sleep problem can now begin. (It will be assumed here that any accompanying medical or psychiatric condition is being appropriately treated.) Assessment has two goals: to clarify the nature of the problem, and to identify which aspects of sleep should be targeted for intervention. Assessment procedures can also be divided into the specific (those which aim to assess the 'dimensions' of the problem), and the general (those which aim to assess aspects of lifestyle which might contribute to the problem, or hinder effective management). Specific aspects of assessment will be considered in this chapter, while general aspects will be considered in *Chapter 8*.

ASSESSING INSOMNIA

In attempting to assess, or quantify, a sleep problem, five characteristics of sleep are of particular relevance:

1 The time taken to get to sleep (sleep onset latency);

2 The total time spent in bed (time in bed);

3 The number of periods of wakefulness intervening during sleep;

4 The duration of periods of wakefulness intervening during sleep;

5 The total amount of time spent asleep (total sleep time, calculated as time in bed minus all the time spent awake).

Each of these characteristics can be estimated from information provided by the client. In order to place the current problem in perspective it is also necessary to obtain: (a) a profile of the client's usual sleep (ie their sleep before the onset of the problem); (b) information concerning recent or relevant changes in sleeping patterns; and (c) an understanding of what, for the client, constitutes the problem. For convenience, much of this information can be collected using the kind of questionnaire shown in the *Appendices* on page 79, and then discussed with the client. Alternatively, these items can be used to structure a face-to-face interview.

Using the Information

The value of much of the information contained in the questionnaire is self-explanatory. From the answers provided it is possible to see whether the client has a sleep onset or a sleep maintenance problem (or both); whether sleep is concentrated at night or distributed throughout the day; how the client sees his or her own sleep; how much sleep the client expects; and whether the problem is new or longstanding. It is also possible to tell just how much time clients spend in bed relative to the amount of time they spend asleep. This can be used to calculate 'sleep efficiency', that is time asleep (in minutes) divided by time in bed (in minutes). The lower this value, the more inefficient the client's sleep.

There are, incidentally, no right or wrong answers. Nevertheless, the following points should assist interpretation of *Sleep Questionnaire* information.

1 Consider sleep onset latency (from Question 2). People vary considerably, but estimated latencies of 30–40 minutes or more (from the time the client settles down to sleep) are reasonable targets for intervention.

2 Consider the overall estimated duration of sleep (either from Question 1 alone, or arithmetically calculated from Questions 8 and 9, with sleep onset latency, night-time wakefulness, and the elapsed time between waking up and getting up deducted). Compare the amount of sleep the client gets with the amount the client expects. Is there a significant mismatch?

3 Consider continuity of sleep. Is the client's sleep broken up by frequent and/or lengthy periods of wakefulness? Persistent night-time awakenings can have a profound impact on sleep quality.

4 Calculate a sleep efficiency score (sleep efficiency = estimated Total Sleep Time divided by estimated Time in Bed). Again, people vary. If the score is 0.6 or less, with substantial periods spent awake before arising, then an earlier getting-up time may be particularly beneficial. Sleep efficiency can be greatly reduced by unsuccessful attempts to 'catch up' on 'lost' sleep.

5 Consider daytime napping. Is it regular or is it haphazard? The latter is nearly always unhelpful.

6 Consider the answers to Questions 14, 15, 17 and 18. How does the client see the problem?

While useful, retrospective questionnaires provide only part of the total picture. Sleep problems occur over time. In order to obtain a broader view of the problem, another type of assessment, serial assessment, is necessary.

Serial Assessment

Serial assessment usually takes the form of self-completed daily ratings. Such ratings not only help to clarify the nature of the problem, but also provide the monitoring necessary for the AIM strategy. The exact amount of detail collected can vary from situation to situation, depending, for example, on the nature of the problem. Small amounts of information can be collected as a graph-type record using the *Daily Sleep Chart* shown in the *Appendices* on page 81. Alternatively, detailed information covering bedtimes and waking frequency (similar to that already collected from the *Sleep Questionnaire*) can be obtained with the more comprehensive *Daily Sleep Diary* (*see Appendices page 82*). Whichever is used, it is essential that the records are completed throughout the period of management, and submitted on at least a weekly basis. In this way daily ratings build into a comprehensive record of day-to-day fluctuations in sleep. For initial assessment purposes, aim to collect at least 10–14 consecutive daily ratings to obtain a clear picture of the client's sleeping patterns.

Serial ratings are well tolerated by clients and, for reasons that are not fully appreciated, can sometimes result in marked improvements in sleep quality. In primary care settings, daily sleep diaries can be returned by post.

Precisely how this information can be used will become clearer in the following chapters. For maximum value, serial assessment should be continued throughout each stage of management.

SUMMARY

The goal of assessment is to clarify the sleep problem and identify possible targets for intervention. Initial assessment should include details of usual sleep, previous sleep problems and the client's perception of the current problem. In addition serial assessment, using daily sleep diaries or charts, can be used both for initial assessment and to monitor the outcome of intervention.

7
Expectations of Sleep

PROVIDING BASIC INFORMATION

So far the client has provided most of the information. Now it's time to reciprocate. Unrealistic expectations of sleep are neither rare nor helpful.
Following the initial assessment, then, it is reasonable to offer the client some basic information on
normal age-related changes in sleep. Some clients
may be unaware that, even for healthy individuals,
sleep becomes shorter, lighter and more broken
with advancing age. Keep in mind that sleep is a
socially inconspicuous activity. Most of us know how
people age on the outside because we experience it
socially. Changes we may experience in ourselves
we also see in others. Sleep, however, tends to be
hidden and consequently prone to misunderstandings. Relevant information on expectations is
provided on the *Sleep Questionnaire* (as already
suggested, contrast the answers to Questions 1 and
12), and may also emerge in an initial face-to-face
interview.

EXPLAINING 'RECOVERY' SLEEP

There is another way in which clients can acquire
unrealistic expectations of sleep. Even for chronic
insomniacs sleep is a self-regulating process. A run

of really dreadful nights may eventually result in the client sleeping for a solid six or seven hours from sheer exhaustion. (If graphed out over several days, such a pattern often emerges from daily sleep diary ratings.) Occasionally, the client may view these untypical 'recovery' nights as their 'normal' sleep. In fact, these occasions of relatively trouble-free sleep are part of the problem, and not a realistic goal for each night. Nevertheless, accumulated sleepiness of the type just described can be put to good use, as explained in *Chapter 9*.

POOR SLEEP AND SHORT SLEEP

At this point attention should also focus quite closely on daytime functioning. In particular, try to discriminate between poor quality sleep (which leaves the client feeling sleepy) and short sleep (which leaves clients alert, but with unwanted time on their hands). The daily sleep records/diaries can help here too. Does the client usually awake feeling reasonably refreshed? Be careful, however, not to dismiss a problem out of hand. Even lifelong short sleepers can develop sleep problems in old age.

It is always useful to reinforce advice with printed material. The issue of ageing and sleep is briefly covered on the *Information for Clients* sheet reproduced in the next chapter.

SUMMARY

Unrealistic expectations of sleep can arise in a number of ways, and are always unhelpful. Common problem areas include unexpected (though normal) changes in the sleep of older persons, the typical sleep patterns of chronic insomnia and confusing short sleep with poor sleep. All should be addressed early in management.

8

Sleep Hygiene

Having assessed the dimensions of the problem it is now appropriate to take a closer look at the client's general habits and behaviours (this can be done during the 10–14 day period when the first serial ratings are accumulating). The goal here is to improve the client's overall 'sleep hygiene'.

WHAT IS SLEEP HYGIENE?

Clinical observations and research findings have identified a variety of behavioural and lifestyle factors which can influence sleep quality. Occasionally such factors represent the sole or major cause of a reported sleep problem. More typically, sleep-disruptive practices tend to interact with, and exacerbate, a more fundamental cause. The aim of sleep hygiene, therefore, is twofold. First, to minimize the impact of disruptive factors on poor sleep and to optimize conditions for improving sleep quality. And second, to provide the basis for future prevention after the main problem responds to management.

OFFERING ADVICE

Advice is useless if the recipient does not see a need

to cooperate (*see Chapter 5*). It is helpful to begin by pointing out, quite simply, that sleep hygiene approaches are clinically effective — and common sense. Once again, it should be explained that the measures suggested are intended to improve sleep quality, and not to cure insomnia. To avoid unnecessary disappointment, it should also be made clear that these measures: (a) are unlikely to improve sleep quality if practised only episodically, and (b) are unlikely to produce benefits within the first one to two weeks.

Don't ask for too much. The needs of the client must always be considered, with sometimes optimal rather than ideal changes agreed. On the other hand be careful not to overcompromise and simply encourage minor and clinically useless changes in personal behaviours.

THRESHOLD EFFECTS

Some poor sleepers are not easily convinced that a life-long habit or practice, previously accompanied by sound sleep, may be contributing to their current problem. Sensitivity to a number of 'sleep antagonists' (eg. caffeine, noise, irregular hours) can change with age and personal circumstances. When sensitivity reaches a critical threshold, sleep is disturbed. It is helpful, therefore, if the operation of threshold effects is explained.

WHERE TO BEGIN

First consider the following points.

1 Chronic poor sleep is frequently accompanied and exacerbated by a corruption of the circadian (24-hour) sleep–wake cycle. To restore and preserve

an optimal 24-hour rhythm in sleep, regular times must be observed for meals, exercise, going to bed, getting up and, if taken, naps.

2 Improvements in the sleep environment can produce improvements in sleep quality. The comfort of the bed, ambient noise and bedroom temperature and ventilation should be considered.

3 Sleep quality can be greatly affected by both alcohol and caffeine, and it is reasonable to focus special attention on these widely used social drugs. While caffeine can delay sleep onset, alcohol can, in certain quantities, disturb sleep in the latter part of the night. Certainly, among poor sleepers, caffeine ingestion should be minimal, while the use of alcohol as a sleep inducer is best avoided.

4 Methodical presleep routines (eg finish cocoa, television off, milk bottles out, cat in, prepare for bed) serve as important behavioural signals for 'winding down' before bed and should be encouraged. Ritual and routine are the guardians of fragile sleep.

5 Weight loss, particularly severe weight loss, can be associated with reductions in sleep quality, and is a frequently overlooked cause of insomnia.

6 It is widely supposed that certain milky drinks contribute to restful sleep. In fact, this is only partly true. If an individual is accustomed to taking milky drinks (or light snacks) close to bedtime, then their sleep might well be a little disturbed if they break this habit. If, on the other hand, a person is unused to snacking late in the evening, then milk drinks or any other food taken at this time might actually disturb their sleep.

7 Regularly scheduled naps can be refreshing and satisfying and are not in themselves a problem. However, napping can be particularly unhelpful if it results from boredom or exhaustion. Under these latter circumstances it will probably have a detrimental impact on night-time sleep.

8 Exercise close to bedtime can produce a state of arousal incompatible with sleep. Exercise, if taken, is probably best avoided in the late evening. The only exception to this is sexual activity which, for a variety of reasons, can actually promote sleep.

9 Prescribed medicines should not be overlooked as a possible cause of sleep problems. In particular some antihypertensives (methyldopa, beta-blockers) can produce sleeplessness and nightmares. Diuretics, too, can remain active at night, and can also cause night-time cramps.

Each of these points provides a possible target for intervention. Decide which are relevant in the present case, and discuss these with the client. A quick check on likely targets can be obtained using the *Sleep Hygiene Checklist* (*see Appendices page 83*).

Finally, advise reasonable change. For example, where sleeping habits have clearly broken down, or where time spent in bed is clearly excessive, bedtimes and getting up times (specifically, times before which the client cannot retire, and after which they cannot stay in bed) can be agreed in the form of a 'contract'. This is explained in *Chapter 9*. General advice covering these points can be accompanied by the information sheet *Getting the Best out of Your Sleep* reproduced below.

INFORMATION FOR CLIENTS I
Getting the Best out of Your Sleep

Whatever the cause of your present sleep problem there are still things you can do that will help you get the most out of your sleep *now*. This sheet is to remind you of the advice you have been given.

1 Don't expect too much from your sleep. As you get older it is quite normal for sleep to become shorter, lighter and more broken. You may also find that your normal sleep routines are more easily disturbed. Rather than changing your sleep, you may need to adjust your expectations and your habits. For example, you may be going to bed too early. Do you really need as much sleep as you think?

2 Because sleep is more easily disturbed in later life, it is best to avoid those things which can prevent or disrupt sleep (even if these things have never been a problem in the past). Learn to take more care of your sleep.

   For example, try drinking less tea or coffee (especially close to bedtime). If you have to get up in the night to go to the toilet, perhaps it is best to avoid late night drinking altogether. You might also consider whether your bed and bedroom are comfortable and quiet enough.

3 It is extremely important to keep regular habits. In particular, avoid excessive daytime napping, or long lie-ins in the morning. Try to keep at least *fairly* active during the day, allowing time to 'wind down' in the evening.

4 If you have a medical complaint that seems to interfere with your sleep (for example, a condition that causes pain or breathlessness at night), see your doctor and explain the problem.

SUMMARY

The goal of sleep hygiene is to identify and modify aspects of lifestyle which might contribute to a sleep problem, or hinder effective management. Within the context of the AIM strategy:

Assess the known problem areas using the *Sleep Hygiene Checklist* (*page 83*);

Intervene by providing information and making realistic suggestions;

Monitor the outcome using daily ratings and verbal feedback from the client.

—9—
Habits and Sleep

Having obtained reasonable improvements in general sleep hygiene, the next practical step is to examine sleep habits in greater detail, and to look for opportunities to improve the *stimulus control* of sleep.

WHAT IS STIMULUS CONTROL?

As with other biological needs (like, for example, eating) sleep has a strong learned component. It is a sound assumption that certain presleep habits and some physical aspects of the sleep environment become so commonly associated with sleep that the very presence of these stimuli helps to promote sleep onset. Getting into bed, for example, can make us feel tired in much the same way as looking at a clock, or sitting at a dinner table can make us feel hungry. Such behaviours are said to be under stimulus control, that is, to a greater or lesser extent these behaviours are influenced by environmental stimuli.

Among chronic insomniacs it is likely that the stimulus control of sleep may be severely weakened by the disintegration of routine, and the prolonged association of the sleep environment with nonsleep-related activities. Chronic poor sleepers can become adept at using their bedrooms for activities which are quite incompatible with sleep. Lying awake night after night it is very tempting to pass the time eating, drinking, smoking, listening to the radio, planning or just worrying. Indeed, it is probable that for some chronic poor sleepers the bedroom actually acquires aversive properties, being more associated with frustration than with rest. Chronic sleep disturbance, then, can lead to the acquisition of new habits which, though unrelated to the onset of insomnia, may nevertheless contribute to its maintenance.

The aim of the stimulus control approach, therefore, is to help the client relearn and benefit from pre-insomnia associations between sleep and the sleep environment. The relearning process has two components: maximizing the opportunity to associate the bed and bedroom with rest and sleep; and minimizing the opportunity to associate the bedroom with any sleep-incompatible behaviours (once again, this can exclude sex). In practice, this means one thing — reducing to a minimum the amount of time spent awake in bed.

WHERE TO BEGIN

Using the initial sleep assessment and accumulated daily sleep diaries or charts, estimate the amount of time the client usually spends in bed, and the amount of this time they usually spend asleep. Discuss these times with the client explaining that, under the circumstances, long periods of time spent awake in bed are detrimental. Then, on the basis of their daily ratings, estimate the amount of sleep per night the client can reasonably expect (this may well be a compromise between what they would like, and what they actually get). Next, negotiate with the client a time of going to bed and getting up sufficient for them to accumulate this agreed amount of sleep (include a reasonable time to fall asleep, say 20–30 minutes).

In addition to the times of going to bed and getting up, four additional rules also need to be discussed.

1 If awake for longer than, say, 20–30 minutes, the client should get up, go to another room, and engage in some reasonably quiet activity (eg. reading or knitting).

2 The client should refrain from any nonsleep-related activity in bed.

3 The client should get up at the agreed time even if tired.

4 The client should avoid napping during the day.

Sometimes it may be necessary to compromise on some of these rules, especially the need to get out of bed in the night. Nevertheless, wherever possible, each should be encouraged. Emphasize that, in insomnia, sleepiness is a precious resource which should not be squandered on unscheduled daytime naps, or extra periods in bed.

At first, the regime may actually reduce total sleep on some nights. This, of course means that the client is more likely to be tired, and consequently more likely to sleep on subsequent nights, and so on. Times for going to bed and getting up can be written onto the *Information for Clients II* sheet reproduced below and given to the client. This sheet can then form a 'contract' between you and the client. It is important, therefore, that the times are mutually agreed.

INFORMATION FOR CLIENTS II
Rules for Improving Sleep Habits

1 Try to go to bed at the same time each night (not too early). _____ (*time*)

2 Try to get up at the same time each morning (not too late). _____ (*time*)

3 When you go to bed try to settle down to sleep as soon as possible.

4 If you have not gone to sleep after about _____ minutes, get up and leave the bedroom until you feel tired again.

5 Try not to read, smoke or listen to the radio etc in bed; *if you can't sleep — get up.*

6 Get up at the agreed time *even if you feel tired or in need of more sleep.* If necessary, set an alarm clock each night.

7 Try to keep active during the day and avoid napping.

8 Go to bed at your usual time and observe the agreed rules.

Stimulus control procedures, combined with appropriate adjustments in sleep hygiene, can be effective within two to three weeks. Monitoring of sleep must, of course, continue throughout this period. Some clients find the procedures difficult, and will need particular encouragement and support. Allow several weeks for sleep to settle down under the new regime before proceeding with further management initiatives.

SUMMARY

The goal of stimulus control procedures is to re-establish or reinforce an association between the sleep environment and sleep itself. Implicitly, this means discouraging an association between the sleep environment and wakefulness, frustration, anxiety and other 'sleep incompatible' activities.

Assess the sleeping habits of the client using information from the *Sleep Questionnaire (page 79)*, daily sleep ratings and interview, and identify appropriate targets for improving stimulus control.

Intervene by explaining the procedure and making reasonable suggestions for change. Provide the client with a list of rules for improving sleep. Negotiate and agree a time of going to bed and getting up.

Monitor the outcome using the daily sleep ratings and verbal feedback from the client.

──────── *10* ────────
Tension and Sleep

In the case of persistent problems, when clients repeatedly experience difficulty in getting off to sleep, or in returning to sleep after waking in the night, there are usually two factors which ultimately deserve closer examination: physical tension and mental tension.

Most people know what it feels like to be physically tense. At such times, we may notice that the muscles in our face, limbs or abdomen are especially tight. Often, we become aware of this tightness because of the discomfort or even pain that it may cause, for example, headaches, aching legs or stomach upsets. Mental tension, on the other hand, refers to those feelings of worry and anxiety often experienced by those who cannot sleep. Worries about the future, thoughts about the day's events, or even anxieties about lack of sleep itself can all contribute to mental tension.

HOW DOES TENSION AFFECT SLEEP?

When it comes to sleep, the brain is a bit like a restaurant waiting to close up. The doors are not usually locked until the last customer has left, so the exact time of closing might vary from night to night. Mental and physical tension are customers who dawdle over coffee, or just refuse to leave, keeping the restaurant open later and later. The metaphor also serves to illustrate a further point. The longer the restaurant stays open, the greater the chance of a new (and unwelcome) customer straying in. Similarly, the more we lie awake (for whatever reason) the more opportunity there is to think and to worry. This, in turn, can prolong wakefulness and the familiar vicious circle develops.

SOME CASE EXAMPLES

Mr A tends to be a worrier, especially when under pressure. He gets butterflies and palpitations, for example, when he is expecting visitors or if he knows he has a lot of jobs to do on a particular day. At such times he notices feeling stiff and restless when he goes to bed, and has trouble getting off to sleep. Invariably, his mind then turns to the following day's events.

Mrs B suffers with arthritic pain affecting her legs and back. She finds that her sleeping is easily disturbed by the pain and that she becomes restless. At such times, she gets increasingly agitated and preoccupied about her loss of sleep.

Mrs C is prone to anxiety at night about various matters such as her health, financial affairs or her family. This seems to keep her awake during the night, and causes her to feel quite weary in the mornings when she rises.

In all of these cases, we can identify a causal link between physical tension (bodily discomfort), and mental tension (what a person is thinking), although the direction of this link may vary. In the case of all of our three clients, however, their thinking pattern has taken on a negative emotional quality, worrying about the next day or about sleep, or just worrying generally. The problem is that this style of thinking produces *arousal*, an alert state incompatible with sleep.

SOURCES OF TENSION

Daytime Tensions

Ordinary daytime events like shopping, queueing, missing buses or having visitors are not without their anxieties and frustrations. These and other apparently trivial situations have the power to 'wind us up', sometimes causing muscular pains or headaches. These may only become noticeable in the evening or at bedtime.

Night-time Tensions

Before going to sleep at night, it is quite normal for thoughts to wander from one topic to another. Often such thoughts are emotionally neutral and harmless. For some people, however, these thoughts can become emotionally charged, converting presleep thoughts into presleep worries. It is worth distinguishing between two very different kinds of worry: anxious worry and depressed worry. Anxious worries — or anxieties — are essentially fear-based thoughts about the future, worries about health, money and so on. Depressed worry, on the other hand, refers to those sad thoughts and reflections concerning, for example, losses of people, places, objects, health or roles.

In order to help clients overcome these stresses it is important to help them identify the different sources of tension which seem to be involved in their particular sleep problem, and then to offer appropriate advice. A structure for doing this is described in the next chapter.

SUMMARY

Physical and mental tensions often underly or accompany chronic sleep-onset problems. Presleep tensions can arise from two quite different types of worry: anxious worry and depressed worry. The management of both types of worry is dealt with in the next chapter.

11

Managing Tension

If the sleep problem appears to be related to tension, then the following six steps can provide a structured response.

Step 1 **RECOGNIZING AND COPING WITH TENSION AS IT ARISES**

Help the client notice which parts of their body get most tense with daily hassles and stress. Some parts of the body may be more affected than others, for example the stomach and face, and (particularly in elderly clients) the arms and shoulders.

Encourage clients to become more aware of which situations usually trigger these physical tensions (eg. rushing, being put under pressure, dealing with people). Help them to observe, too, from an actual example in their daily repertoire, how certain characteristic ways of thinking may be the cause of physical tension. If they are habitually worrying about things, encourage them to judge whether, on balance, such worrying has any benefits.

Step 2 **CREATING A WORRY PERIOD**

If mental tension appears to have become a significant feature of a client's night-time pattern, remind the client that this is likely to be detrimental to sleep. If necessary create a 'worry buffer'. Suggest to clients that they should set aside a period of time during the day for worrying. This simple procedure has two consequences. First, it gives the client *permission* to worry (people often feel guilty about worrying). And second, it encourages the client to deal with worries one at a time. This type of scheduled worrying may seem strange to the client at first, so initial supervised practice is essential. The following form of words may be helpful when explaining the procedure.

"Most people realize that they can do their jobs better if they leave domestic and family problems at home. Of course, at the end of the day the problems are still there, but at least they haven't been nagging away and interfering with work. There is nothing unusual, therefore, about setting problems aside for the time being, and picking them up later. You can apply the same principle to sleep. Instead of worrying when you get to bed, confine your worrying thoughts to a regular time each day. Write your worries down in a notebook so that you can remember what to worry about. You will be surprised how this can clarify things, and you will probably notice how the same problems crop up time and time again."

Step 3 **SELF-QUESTIONING**

If the client is troubled by intrusive thoughts which seem to maintain a disturbed sleep pattern, encourage them to practise and learn the following self-questioning routine. Reassure the client that, while the routine may appear simplistic, there are times when we all need to apply simple logic to our personal worries.

Each time you find yourself worrying at night, ask yourself the following:

1 "Am I an anxious person? Do I worry about most things?" If the answer to this is 'yes', then you will probably know by now that things turn out no better for worrying.

2 "Am I worrying about one thing or several?" Remember that, if you worry about several things at the same time, it is highly unlikely that you will come to any useful conclusion.

3 "Am I worrying about something of real importance?" If this is the case (and often it is not), then you must give some attention to this matter.

4 "Is it a problem that I can actually do something about?" If there is a solution to your problem, attend to it as soon as is reasonable and stop worrying.

5 "Is it a problem that can wait until morning?" Often it is, so make a daytime appointment with yourself to think about it a bit more.

6 "Is the problem making me feel tense and on edge?" If the answer is 'yes', you should be applying some relaxation to your body.

Step 4 FIGHTING FEAR

Being startled at night by a sudden and unexpected noise can cause anxieties even in the bravest person. When this happens our nervous system becomes hyperactive, and our minds can run wild. These emergency reactions are quite normal. Among older people who may feel especially vulnerable, however, such reactions may be more persistent. Encourage clients who are particularly disturbed by such worries to bring themselves into check using a relaxation method. Of course, it is also important to encourage the client to take all reasonable steps to secure their home before going to bed.

Step 5 **COPING WITH DEPRESSED THOUGHTS**

During periods of night-time wakefulness it is quite common for people to dwell on the ups and downs of their life, sometimes with an emphasis on the downs. Many people who have reached retirement age have lived through periods of great personal distress, involving illness, losses or bereavement. These down thoughts can arise with a particular intensity at night.

Of course, at times of personal loss it is quite normal to experience periods of depression. Depression can have a marked effect on sleep, and often produces early morning wakening. If, in your view, the client's primary problem is depression, or the depression is evidently severe, then it is important to encourage the client to seek appropriate specialist help.

Notwithstanding the advice just given, there are therapeutic strategies which can help the client whose sleep is disturbed by stressful and painful thoughts. Particularly useful are simplified cognitive therapy routines which encourage clients to consider whether their thoughts are realistic or unduly negative. Clients can then be helped to identify alternative, more positive, thoughts about their situation. These methods, which require considerable skill, will be considered in the next chapter.

Step 6 UNDERSTANDING AND TEACHING RELAXATION

The ability to relax is not something that can be taken for granted. For example, while most people are able to wind down on holiday or at other special times, many find it difficult to relax in the course of a normal day. Nevertheless, relaxing is a fairly simple skill that can be learned at any age.

Research shows that, on average, relaxation can reduce periods of sleeplessness by half. There are a variety of different techniques. Increasingly, clients themselves may have had some previous experience with one or another of these methods. It helps if we can see these techniques as falling into two groups. On the one hand, there are methods which emphasize physical manipulation such as massage and selective muscle tension. On the other hand, there are methods that emphasize a mental approach utilizing thoughts and imagery. Whichever method is chosen, it is important that relaxation is taught and not prescribed.

What is it about relaxation that is helpful to sleep? There are three ingredients of relaxation which seem to be active. First, there is a direct physiological effect which, through muscle-tone reduction, alleviates such sleep-inhibiting factors as postural tension and pain. Second, by focusing the mind on somatic or other sensations we are effectively displacing intrusive thoughts which can delay or prevent sleep onset. And third, the pleasant, monotonous rhythmic pattern of relaxation itself appears to be soporific.

Clearly, there is a need to tailor the relaxation method to the particular circumstances of the individual, promoting wherever possible the best combination of these effects. In general, the method of progressive muscular relaxation appears to promote all three (it directly involves the release of tension from muscles, it employs a dialogue that directs the mind to pleasant bodily sensations, and it has a paced regularity). On the other hand, older clients, who may have problems with arthritis or cramp, may find this method troublesome. An alternative for such clients would be autogenic relaxation, which misses out the actual physical tensing and focuses on imagined sensations of relaxation.

Clients can be taught an appropriate technique singly or in groups. For continued practice at home the use of audiotapes is particularly useful. It is important, however, that the tape should be accompanied by clear instructions, examples of which are provided below (*Information for Clients III*).

SUMMARY

Presleep worries and anxieties can, by increasing tension, delay sleep onset, and prevent a satisfactory return to sleep following night-time awakenings. Several strategies are suggested here for helping clients to cope with, and overcome, sources of tension.

Assess the kinds of anxiety the client may have through face-to-face interview.

Intervene by introducing the client to the steps (suggested in this chapter) for addressing and preventing tension at night. An appropriate relaxation technique can also be taught. Remember, however, that relaxation must be taught and not prescribed.

Monitor the client's response using daily ratings, verbal feedback and your own judgement.

INFORMATION FOR CLIENTS III
Relaxation and Sleep: How to Prepare Yourself

It will help you best if you practise these exercises at least twice each day; preferably once in the morning before you start your day properly (make a regular time if possible), and then again at night-time when you have settled down ready to try and sleep. If you experience difficulties with getting back to sleep in the night, you should also use the relaxation to help you at these times.

In the daytime you may relax on your bed or in a chair. Make sure that your arms, legs and head are supported properly before you begin. Ensure that you are in the room on your own and that other members of your family will not disturb you.

To begin with, practice by using the taped relaxation instructions both in the morning and at night. Don't be too ambitious. If the exercises help you to relax only a little, that is a start. You can expect things to get better with practice. Do not expect any dramatic changes in your sleep pattern. Remember what you are aiming for is to be more relaxed whether you are awake or asleep.

When you get more confident of what is involved in the relaxation exercise, try managing once or twice without the tape. After two or three weeks, you should be able to relax on some occasions without using the tape. See how you get on and discuss with your sleep adviser any particular difficulties you are experiencing at an early stage so that they can be sorted out immediately.

You don't have to stick to the exact same wording; you may find a form of words that is comfortable for you. It is important though to maintain a regular rhythm throughout and to focus in turn on all the different parts of your body.

12

Thoughts and Sleep

Some clients seem to have a problem controlling their presleep thoughts and find it difficult to get into the right frame of mind for going to sleep. For these people relaxation may work because, by providing a focus of attention, it prevents or blocks the typically exaggerated, unrealistic, irrational and uniformly negative thoughts which can delay sleep onset. An alternative way of dealing with these same thoughts, after other methods have been used to their best advantage, is to use a simplified form of cognitive therapy. The aim here is not to block thoughts but to meet them head-on, learn to recognize them for what they are, challenge them, and ultimately replace them with more reassuring and rational alternatives. The approach requires careful preparation and, in circumstances of marked depression or anxiety, the application of this or any other therapy should be left to those with appropriate expertise. This chapter, then, is intended both for those relatively unfamiliar with the ideas of cognitive therapy, and for those who may be accustomed to the technique, but who may be unaccustomed to its use in the management of poor sleep.

COGNITIVE THERAPY FOR POOR SLEEP

Cognitive therapy is based upon rather simple but important understandings about the source of emotions, such as anxiety, depression and anger. First it is recognized that all emotions follow on from the thoughts we have. Second, people can sometimes be 'wound-up' by apparently 'realistic' thoughts which, if subjected to closer examination, can be recognized by the client as being unrealistic. The aims of the therapy are to help clients to: (a) identify their thinking patterns, (b) recognize a link between their thoughts and their emotions, (c) become more familiar with the bias in their thinking, and (d) learn to correct this bias by rehearsing and practising alternative ways of thinking about situations.

The cognitive therapy procedures outlined below are designed to be introduced over three sessions, each separated by at least two weeks. In the first two sessions the client is introduced to the technique in a graduated way, and encouraged to practise at home. In the final session the overall success of training is assessed, any misunderstandings are ironed out, and final encouragement given. Monitoring of sleep, using the *Daily Sleep Diary* (*page 82*), is continued throughout (additional questions relating to the frequency of intrusive thoughts can be added). The content of the first two sessions is reinforced using the information sheets reproduced below, which also provide a detailed overview of session structure.

INFORMATION FOR CLIENTS IV

Thoughts and Sleep: Step 1

Whether preoccupied with the past, ruminating on the present or anticipating the future, our thoughts affect how we feel and what we do. For example, consider Mr A, an elderly widower who is used to sharing a holiday each year with his son's family. This year they haven't invited him. What might he think?

"Maybe they are fed up with me always being around. I must be boring company for them. Have I done something to offend them? They have stopped caring about me."

OR "They have been considerate to take me with them in the past. I can understand that they need time together as a family. Maybe it's good for me to know I can manage without them."

If he believes this chain of thoughts he would probably feel sad, angry or puzzled. He may even feel like avoiding his family or become irritable in their company and whenever such thoughts revisit him.

If he believes this chain of thoughts he is less likely to feel upset. He may even feel pleased for not putting himself first.

Consider a further example:
Mr A has now been asked by a relatively new acquaintance to go on holiday together. What might he think?

"I'm not sure what I'm committing myself to. We might have different tastes. We might not get on. What if we were to fall out?"

OR "I'm reluctant to go on holiday alone. Perhaps this is a good opportunity for me. We might get on well. I am still free to make up my own mind about the things I would like to do."

If he believes this chain of thoughts he would probably feel anxious and keep dwelling on the things that could go wrong, even worrying that it could end up disastrously. These thoughts might well disrupt his sleep.

OR

If he believes this chain of thoughts he is more likely to feel comforted, even pleased. These thoughts will not prevent him from going to sleep.

Remember:
What you say to yourself affects how you feel and what you do. The things you say to yourself at night-time can make you emotionally aroused and keep you awake. Once started, these chains of thoughts are very difficult to stop, and you may find yourself becoming more anxious, sad or angry. So by stopping the spiral of these unpleasant and unhelpful thoughts at times when you are in bed, you can encourage a more restful sleep.

How to stop disruptive thoughts and improve your sleep: Step 1

First, you must learn to identify your disruptive thoughts so that you can challenge them. Often these thoughts, which are called *negative* thoughts, will have one or more of the following features:

1 They are automatic and habitual; they just seem to pop up without any effort on your part.

2 They are irrational or distorted: they do not always fit the facts.

3 They are exaggerated: they tend to overestimate the danger or difficulty.

4 They are unhelpful: they keep you anxious, depressed or angry.

5 They are plausible: it may not occur to you to question them.

6 They are involuntary: they can be very difficult to 'switch off'.

7 They are defeatist: they presume you cannot possibly cope.

Here are some examples of how these negative thoughts might be used:

"I will never be able to do it ..."
"It's terrible ..."
"This is dangerous ..."
"What if I can't ..."
"I won't have time ..."
"I'll look stupid ..."
"I'm a failure ..."
"I just know nobody likes me ..."

At first you may not find it easy to catch your automatic thoughts, but with practice it will become more natural. Once you have learned to spot a negative thought, you can then learn to provide yourself with an alternative which is more realistic and positive.

How to practise

1 Set aside 25 minutes each evening to make a record of your thoughts. Do this at least two hours before going to bed.

2 Write down everything you can remember thinking in bed last night. Try to record these as accurately as possible. Write them down word for word if you can. If your thoughts take the form of pictures rather than words, write down what you saw in your 'mind's eye'.

3 Now examine each thought you have written down. Is it realistic? Can you think of something to replace it with? What would you say to a friend with this thought? Write your conclusions down in the next column, and decide how much you believe in the thought now.

Beware of excuses which keep you from focusing on your thoughts or writing your diary. It is quite natural to avoid recalling unpleasant thoughts or experiences. However, doing so is one of the best ways of controlling an overactive mind, and encouraging restful sleep.

INFORMATION FOR CLIENTS V
Thoughts and Sleep: Step 2

What you say to yourself, your impressions and thoughts, can affect how you feel and what you do. Certain negative thoughts can help to keep you awake. If this happens you can improve your sleep first by identifying these negative thoughts, and then by changing them.

At our last meeting we discussed the first step: identifying negative thoughts. This summary considers the next step: changing negative thoughts.

How to stop disruptive thoughts and improve your sleep: Step 2

Once you have identified the thoughts, ask yourself several questions.

1 What is the evidence?

   (a) Am I confusing thought with fact? Just because you believe something to be true doesn't mean it is true.

   (b) Am I jumping to conclusions? If you are, then you are basing your conclusions on poor evidence.

   (c) Examine the evidence for your particular thought. What evidence do you have to back it up? Do you know anything that might contradict your thought? Do you think this particular thought would be accepted by other people?

2 What alternatives are there?

   (a) What is the evidence to support an alternative thought?

   (b) How do you think another person would see things?

   (c) What would you say to another person if they told *you* about this thought?

After examining the thought and producing an alternative, try to think of a statement which will reassure you and help you to think in a more positive way. By doing this you can stop the thoughts which keep you awake.

Here are some examples of positive things we can say to ourselves:

"There will be plenty of time …"
"I'm sure it will be OK, it always has been in the past …"
"I won't dwell on it, it doesn't help …"
"I'll be able to sort it out …"
"Just relax, it won't be that bad …"

Write down any others you can think of:

_____

Notice the difference between these positive thoughts, and the negative thoughts described in the previous summary.

Remember:
Negative automatic thoughts are seldom based on any evidence, and there is usually a better alternative.

So:
Identify your automatic negative thoughts.
Question whether they are sensible and realistic.
Try to replace them with alternative, more rational, thoughts.
Find a positive statement which reassures you.

How to practise

1 Set aside 25 minutes each evening and repeat the exercises you carried out after the last session.
2 This time, examine each thought and ask yourself the questions already described: what is the evidence? what are the alternatives?
3 Having worked through the above steps you should now produce a short positive statement which reassures you. Make sure it is one you can believe. If you can't find one, go back and examine the original thought again; look at the evidence and produce an alternative.

When you go to bed at night you may find you have thoughts which you have already worked on during the day. If so, remember the positive reassuring statement you produced. Even if it is a new thought you will probably be able to use these reassuring statements. Try repeating them to yourself while thinking of a pleasant relaxing scene. You will probably find that the thought does not come into your mind again and sleep will shortly follow. If your reassuring statement *doesn't* reassure you, then you will have to work through the thought again as you did in the exercise during the day.

Remember:
Learning to influence your negative thoughts takes time and practice. Don't expect immediate improvements in your sleep; these improvements will come as you become more familiar with the technique.

SUMMARY

Certain styles of presleep thinking can delay sleep onset, and have a generally detrimental influence on sleep quality. In addition to the improved sleep hygiene and relaxation described in earlier chapters, simplified cognitive therapy strategies can improve sleep onset problems by helping the client to deal more effectively with disruptive presleep thoughts.

Assess the client's usual 'style' of thinking when awake at night. Is it likely that this type of thinking is delaying sleep onset? Is the client aware of a connection between thoughts and sleep? Encourage the client to keep a diary of presleep thoughts.

Intervene by explaining the link between thoughts and feelings; teach clients to recognize any bias in their thinking; introduce clients to alternative ways of thinking about the situations on which they dwell.

Monitor the client's response using daily ratings, verbal feedback, and your own judgement.

─── *13* ───
Sleep-related Behaviours

Given the steady increase in sleep problems seen in later life it is perhaps comforting that many of the more disturbing sleep-related behaviours like sleep-walking, sleeptalking and night terrors actually become less common with increasing age. There are, nevertheless, three particular sleep-related behaviours which do become more prevalent in later life, and all have implications for sleep quality. These are snoring, limb movements in sleep and cramps.

SNORING

Clinical attitudes towards snoring have changed considerably in the past 10 years. Once viewed as a relatively benign though irritating activity, snoring is increasingly being seen as an important 'marker' for several medical conditions, the most notable of which is obstructive sleep apnoea. In this condition the muscles of the throat gradually relax as the individual falls deeper into sleep, causing some respiratory distress. Eventually the airway blocks altogether, and breathing stops. Oxygen deprived, the sleeper is aroused to lighter sleep (though may not be aware of 'waking up'), gasps and splutters as the airway clears, and the cycle begins again.

One effect of this process is that, very often, sleep-apnoeic individuals are very sleepy during the day, but don't know why. Sleep apnoea tends to be more common among men than women, among fat rather than thin people, among elderly rather than younger people, and more common among elderly people with dementia than elderly people without dementing illness.

As regards age, sex and obesity, snoring shows a similar pattern of relationships. The tendency to snore increases with age, affecting up to 40 per cent of middle-aged women, and 60 per cent of middle-aged men. It is also more likely to affect the overweight. The actual clinical relevance of all these relationships is, however, far from clear. Certainly, elderly people who snore do not necessarily have a life-threatening sleep apnoea syndrome. Nevertheless, if snoring is associated with excessive daytime sleepiness, then it should be medically investigated.

As the tendency to snore is exacerbated by obesity, alcohol, smoking and posture (lying on the back), it makes sense to address each of these factors if the behaviour is a nuisance either for the snorer or for listeners.

LIMB MOVEMENTS

For reasons that are not at all clear, limb movements during sleep also become more common with increasing age. Two related conditions can cause particular distress, either for the bed partner or for the sufferer: periodic movements in sleep, and the restless leg syndrome. Periodic movements in sleep (PMS) refers to sudden kicking movements made during sleep which, though sometimes quite violent, may not wake up the kicker. Conversely, in the restless leg syndrome, the sufferer is aware of an unpleasant 'pins and needles' sensation in the legs which can only be relieved by jerky movements. There is some evidence that these conditions can respond to drug therapy, but there is no widely agreed specific treatment.

CRAMPS

Severe limb cramps are also particularly common in old age but, unlike PMS or restless legs, can be managed quite successfully with drugs, usually quinine sulphate. Remember also that cramps can result from diuretic therapy.

—————14—————
Caring Through the Night

Much of the advice and information offered so far assumes that the client has presented with the sleep problem, and has also agreed to participate in its management. There are situations within caring relationships, however, where either or both of these assumptions do not hold. For example, within residential settings where the care staff may observe and report the sleep problem. Or in the case of severe dementing illness where the sufferer is no longer able to consent or cooperate.

Under these circumstances the AIM strategy can still be applied, but in a different way. In particular, both assessment and intervention have to be especially cautious. This chapter, then, outlines a structured approach to the management of sleep in residential or hospital settings where the needs of elderly people are met by professional carers. Much of the information presented will apply equally to informal carers, and can therefore be used as advice for those caring at home.

MANAGING THE SLEEP OF DEPENDENT ELDERLY PEOPLE: 10 POINTS TO CONSIDER

1 When responding to the apparently poor sleep of other people the first thing to consider is

whether they *really* have a sleep problem. Don't, for example, confuse short sleep or broken sleep with poor sleep. If the sleep problem has been reported by care staff, ensure, if possible, that the client shares these perceptions. Try to find out if sleep is more disturbed than before admission or the onset of a present illness.

2 Is the bedroom comfortable and quiet enough? Remember that elderly people are more easily awakened by noise. Try to anticipate, and rectify if possible, sources of discomfort (extremes of temperature, poor ventilation, etc). Make sure the bed itself is comfortable. Could the client be made more comfortable if provided with additional equipment (special pillows, bed-frames, etc)?

3 Remember that individuals differ enormously in terms of the amounts of sleep they need and when they need it. On admission enquire about the client's usual sleep habits and, as far as possible, try to accommodate it. Try to allow for flexible times of going to bed and getting up. If the client is confined to bed, try to avoid turning the lights out too early. High levels of physical activity are not a prerequisite for tiredness, and even relatively immobile people get sleepy around their usual bedtime.

4 Try to deal constructively with periods of night-time awakening. If the client habitually wakes up in the night, is there anything for them to do? An unsympathetic or inflexible response to a client's behaviour can create an *apparent* sleep problem. Consider, for example, an elderly person who, for the past 20 years has satisfactorily coped with periods of wakefulness at home by reading, or making a cup of tea. If these

diversions are made unavailable, the client is left with nothing to fill their wakefulness, which now becomes a problem.

Naturally, it would be counter-productive actively to encourage night-time activities (*see Chapter 9*). Nevertheless, time spent in some harmless diversion is preferable to a lengthy period of boredom for someone who has long since adjusted to changed sleep patterns.

5 If the client is likely to be confused, make sure there is a night-light. When awake darkness can add to confusion and cause fear.

6 If a sleep problem persists, make it the subject of an interdisciplinary discussion or case conference. There may be an underlying and treatable cause or other management possibilities which emerge from this broader discussion.

7 One of the most important considerations when looking after the sleep of others is to maintain the difference between night and day. It is very easy (and, in the case of elderly confused and dementing clients, very tempting) passively to encourage sleep during the day among those who are awake, and perhaps disruptive during the night. Indeed, after a sleepless night most people, with or without dementing illness, need little encouragement to fall asleep during the day. People who sleep during the day are less likely to sleep during the night, and vice versa. Bit by bit this vicious circle can affect sleep–wake patterns to the point where a person may be asleep for much of the day, but awake for much of the night.

8 While some drugs can contribute to, or cause, insomnia, others have the unintentional side-effect of causing drowsiness. For example, some

antidepressants, pain-killers, antihistamines and cough medicines can actually produce feelings of sleepiness. If such drugs are currently being taken, then it can make good sense to take one of the prescribed doses last thing at night in order to exploit their sedative effects. In addition, medicines which relieve specific symptoms (for example inhalations which relieve breathlessness) might also be taken last thing at night in order to maximize the benefit.

9 If the client's sleep has become very disorganized than a very short course of sleeping tablets might help restore a more natural day–night routine. This would involve taking the tablet at an appropriate bedtime and then, during the following day, providing sufficient stimulation to maintain wakefulness until the next bedtime. If repeated for several nights, sleep can be 'retimed'. The emphasis here is on a 'short course' of tablets, say three to four nights at the most. Note, however, that sleeping tablets can cause or worsen confusion in susceptible frail elderly people.

10 Finally, many of the sleep hygiene and stimulus control procedures described above are suitable for frail or confused elderly people. If you are in control of the sleep environment, then you are also in control of a major influence on sleep quality.

SUMMARY

Two basic principles should guide the management of sleep in hospital or residential settings: identify and avoid things which can counteract sleep; and encourage those things which promote sleep. In order to identify targets for intervention a structured process of review is recommended. In particular, where sleep is identified as a special problem the care team should assess the client's daily and nightly routines, the sleep environment, the style of care provided, and the possible impact of specific components of treatment. In all caring environments special attention should focus on the maintenance of regular personal schedules and on maximizing feelings of healthy sleepiness.

15
What About Sleeping Tablets?

Over the past 30 years or so, the prescribing of tablets for sleep complaints has become quite commonplace. Because complaints of poor sleep tend to increase with age, it is also the case that, as a rule, elderly people consume the lion's share of these tablets. However, it is also becoming increasingly clear that prescribing drugs is not the ideal solution to insomnia in old age. Indeed, far from providing a solution, these drugs often become part of the problem.

While sleeping tablets can be extremely useful in the treatment of some types of sleep disturbance, there are many disadvantages associated with their use. Some of the questions people often ask about the effects and the side-effects of sleeping tablets are answered below.

WHAT ARE SLEEPING TABLETS?

Sleeping tablets are sedative drugs which produce feelings of tranquillity and drowsiness. Medically, these drugs are referred to as 'hypnotics' (from the Greek word *hypnos* meaning sleep). Most modern sleeping tablets belong to a group of drugs called 'benzodiazepines'. Drugs of this type can be recognized by their names, which usually end in 'pam' or 'am' (for example, nitrazepam, temazepam, triazolam).

ARE SLEEPING TABLETS SIMILAR TO TRANQUILLIZERS?

For the most part sleeping tablets are the *same* as tranquillizers. Both usually belong to the same group of drugs (ie benzodiazepines), both reduce anxiety, and both can be used to promote sleep in the short term. When used as tranquillizers, however, benzodiazepines are used in doses which do not induce sleep.

ARE THERE ANY OTHER TYPES OF SLEEPING TABLETS?

Yes. Before the introduction of benzodiazepines the barbiturates were very popular (eg. phenobarbitone, amylobarbitone). These are now rarely prescribed for sleep problems, but may still be used by some older people. In hospitals, the drug chlormethiazole is often used to treat sleep problems in elderly in-patients, while some general practitioners show a preference for the drug chloral hydrate when treating insomnia among elderly people at home. For the most part all of these drugs share the same advantages and disadvantages as the benzodi-azepines. More recently the drug zopiclone has been introduced; this drug appears to promote sleep, yet avoids some of the nastier long-term side-effects of benzodiazepines. At present, experience of this drug is rather limited, particularly among elderly people.

WHAT DO SLEEPING TABLETS DO TO SLEEP?

An effective sleeping tablet will reduce the length of time it takes to get off to sleep, reduce the number of awakenings during the night, and increase the total amount of time spent asleep. Most sleeping tablets will also reduce the amount of time spent in REM sleep, thus diminishing or eliminating vivid dreams.

DO SLEEPING TABLETS BECOME LESS EFFECTIVE WITH REPEATED USE?

Yes. It is now widely accepted that most sleeping tablets become less effective after about 14 days of continuous usage.

ARE SLEEPING TABLETS APPROPRIATE FOR ALL TYPES OF INSOMNIA?

No. Sleeping tablets are of value *mainly* in the treatment of very short-term insomnias where the cause of the problem is known, and the sleep disturbance is severe, disabling or subjects the individual to extreme distress.

DO SLEEPING TABLETS HAVE ANY SIDE EFFECTS?

Yes, especially in older people. The effects of some sleeping drugs can persist into the next day causing drowsiness, impaired coordination, memory problems, disturbed concentration and sometimes confusion. Sleeping drugs can also affect mood, and might lead to uncharacteristic outbursts of anger or an increased tendency to worry during the day.

ARE SLEEPING TABLETS ADDICTIVE?

Yes. Even if taken in normal doses under medical supervision it is possible to become 'dependent' on sleeping tablets. Dependency means that, if the tablets are abruptly discontinued, the individual will experience a number of unpleasant withdrawal effects. Ironically these withdrawal effects, which disappear if the drug is recommenced, include disturbed sleep and insomnia. Consequently, many people continue to take sleeping tablets for long periods of time just to avoid these withdrawal symptoms.

16

Managing Sleep and Insomnia

WHOSE RESPONSIBILITY?

On the assumption that first steps are often the most difficult, this final section will briefly consider the issue of 'where to begin?'. Interestingly, the value of this particular question lies not in its answer (which is 'at the beginning', to quote the King of Hearts again) but in the attention it draws to the related, but frequently overlooked issue of '*who* should begin?'. Throughout this book considerable emphasis has been placed on an interdisciplinary approach to management involving all those with a professional interest in the care of older people. But who should take initial responsibility?

It is interesting, and useful, to consider this question in a broader context. One of the more subtle 'side-effects' of hypnotic drugs is that they have helped to define, narrowly and perhaps unfairly, who should take responsibility for sleep problems. It is reasonable to suggest, then, that insomnia (at any age) has tended to be seen, both by the clients and by many professionals, as the responsibility of prescribing doctors. Clearly, however, where the management of a client's sleep problem is shared, responsibility for that problem is also shared. So, in answer to the question 'who should begin?', the answer is simple enough: *the first health care professional to encounter the problem* (whether the initial response is to alert others to the problem, or to refer the client on to another agency, or to mobilize colleagues in addressing the problem, or to commence a detailed programme of assessment). Sleep problems in later life are unlikely to receive the attention they deserve if they are consistently seen as someone else's responsibility.

Encouraging a broader responsibility for identifying and managing the sleep problems of older clients will, of course, require some adjustment in professional attitudes and practices. A broadening of responsibility will, it is hoped, accompany the more widespread deployment of the management strategies suggested here. It is also hoped that, ultimately, recognition of sleep problems and the opportunities for effective intervention and management will find a permanent place in the education and training of therapists, clinicians and professional carers.

Appendices

———Further Reading———

The books and review articles selected below are intended as source references. The specific studies are included as useful examples of current research. Collectively this literature describes the research and clinical basis for much of the information provided in this book.

BOOKS AND REVIEW ARTICLES

On sleep

Oswald I, *Sleep*, Penguin, Harmondsworth, 1980.
Horne J, *Why we Sleep*, Oxford University Press, Oxford, 1988.

On Sleep in Later Life

Morgan K, *Sleep and Ageing: A Research Based Guide to Sleep in Later Life*, Chapman and Hall, London, 1987.

On the Management of Insomnia

Borkovec TD, 'Insomnia', *Journal of Consulting and Clinical Psychology* 50, pp880–895, 1982.
Lacks P, *Behavioural Treatment for Persistent Insomnia*, Pergamon, New York, 1987.

On the Insomnias and Other Sleep Disorders

Williams R & Karacan I (eds), *Sleep Disorders: Diagnosis and Treatment,* 2nd Edn, Wiley, New York, 1988.

On Sleeping Tablets

Morgan K, 'Hypnotics in the Elderly: What Cause for Concern?' *Drugs* 40(5), pp688–696, 1990.

RESEARCH STUDIES ON THERAPY FOR INSOMNIA

Puder R, Lacks P, Bertelson AD & Storandt M, 'Short-term Stimulus Control Treatment of Insomnia in Older Adults', *Behavior Therapy* 14, pp424–429, 1983.

Schoicket SL, Bertelson AD & Lacks P, 'Is Sleep Hygiene a Sufficient Treatment for Sleep-Maintenance Insomnia?', *Behavior Therapy* 19, pp183–190, 1988.

Lacks P & Powlishta K, 'Improvement Following Behavioural Treatment for Insomnia: Clinical Significance, Long-term Maintenance, and Predictors of Outcome,' *Behavior Therapy* 20, pp117–134, 1989.

Espie CA, Lindsay WR & Brooks DN, 'Substituting Behavioural Treatment for Drugs in the Treatment of Insomnia: An Exploratory Study', *Journal of Behaviour Therapy and Experimental Psychiatry* 19, pp51–56, 1988.

Espie CA, Lindsay WR, Brooks DN, Hood EM & Turvey T, 'A Controlled Comparative Investigation of Psychological Treatments for Chronic Sleep Onset Insomnia', *Behaviour Research and Therapy* 27, pp79–88, 1989.

—Sleep Questionnaire—

Below are some questions concerning your sleep. Please answer all the questions. If your times for going to bed and so on vary greatly, give ranges (eg. 10–11pm, 30–60 mins)

1	For how long do you usually sleep at night?		
2	After settling down, how long does it usually take you to fall asleep?		
3	How often do you wake up too early in the morning? (tick one):	Never Seldom Sometimes Often All the time	☐ ☐ ☐ ☐ ☐
4	Do you usually wake up during the night?	Yes No	☐ ☐
5	If Yes: What usually awakes you? (answer in your own words)		
6	How many times (on average) do you awake each night?		
7	For how long are you awake on each of these occasions?		
8	At what time do you usually go to bed?		
9	At what time do you usually wake up (in the morning)?		

10	At what time do you usually get up?		
11	How refreshed do you usually feel when you wake up in the morning (tick one)?	Very refreshed Quite refreshed Unrefreshed Tired Shattered	☐ ☐ ☐ ☐ ☐
12	In general, how much sleep do you think a person your age needs?		
13	How long have you had your present sleep problem?		
14	What do you think is the cause of your present sleep problem? (answer in your own words)		
15	Have you ever had serious trouble with your sleep in the past?	Yes No	☐ ☐
16	Have you gained or lost weight in the last few months? (tick one)	Yes, I have gained weight Yes, I have lost weight No, I'm about the same	☐ ☐ ☐
17	Before the present problem how would you have described yourself (tick one):	A very good sleeper A good sleeper An average sleeper A poor sleeper A very poor sleeper	☐ ☐ ☐ ☐ ☐
18	How would you describe yourself now?	A very good sleeper A good sleeper An average sleeper A poor sleeper A very poor sleeper	☐ ☐ ☐ ☐ ☐
19	Do you usually take a nap during the day?	Yes No	☐ ☐
20	When do you usually nap? (give length of each nap)		

Thank you for completing this questionnaire.

Daily Sleep Chart

		1	2	3	4	5	6	7	8	9	10	11	12	13	14	15
Sleep latency (minutes)	120+															
	60															
	50															
	40															
	30															
	20															
	10															
Total sleep (hours)	8+															
	7															
	6															
	5															
	4															
	3															
	2															
	1															
Sleep quality	Very good															
	Good															
	Average															
	Poor															
	Very Poor															
Day		1	2	3	4	5	6	7	8	9	10	11	12	13	14	15
Start Date																

——Daily Sleep Diary——

Name		Date
1	At what time did you go to bed last night?	
2	At what time did you settle down to sleep?	
3	How long did it take you to fall asleep?	
4	How many times did you wake up?	
5	What woke you up?	
6	For how long do you think you were awake on each of these occasions?	
7	At what time did you finally wake up?	
8	How did you feel when you woke up this morning? (tick one)	Refreshed and alert ☐ Alert but not at peak ☐ Tired ☐ Absolutely shattered ☐
9	At what time did you get up?	
10	How would you rate last night's sleep? (tick one)	Very Good ☐ Good ☐ Average ☐ Poor ☐ Very Poor ☐
11	What medicines did you take yesterday?	
12	How much alcohol did you drink yesterday?	

Sleep Hygiene Checklist

Each score of *1* indicates an area of special concern	Yes	No
Does the client maintain fairly regular habits (eg. bedtimes, getting-up times, mealtimes)?	0	1
Could the client's bedroom be quieter or more comfortable?	1	0
Does the client drink caffeinated drinks close to bedtime or during the night?	1	0
Does the client use alcohol as a sleep inducer?	1	0
Does the client have an identifiable presleep routine?	0	1
Does the client nap habitually?	1	0
Is the client usually tired on retiring?	0	1
Is the client choosing when to go to bed?	0	1
Is the client usually tired/sleepy during the day?	1	0
Is the client taking any prescribed medicine with known disruptive effects on sleep?	1	0